STEVE REICH

CELLO COUNTERPOINT

(version for Solo Cello and Tape)

Solo Cello Part

HENDON MUSIC

BOOSEY & HAWKES

DISTRIBUTED BY

HAL•LEONARD®
7777 W. BLUEMOUND RD. P.O. BOX 13819 MILWAUKEE, WI 53213

www.boosey.com
www.halleonard.com

Note by the Composer

Cello Counterpoint (2003) is scored for eight cellos, and can be played by a soloist with the other parts pre-recorded. This tape is available from the Boosey & Hawkes rental library. Alternately, the piece can be played by a Cello Octet. Please note that there are differences in distribution of parts between the version for Solo Cello and Tape and the version for Cello Octet, including Cello 1. A separate set of materials (including parts for making your own backing track, if desired) is used when performing the Solo Cello and Tape version.

Cello Counterpoint is in three movements: fast, slow, fast. The first and last movements are both based on a similar four-chord cycle that moves ambiguously back and forth between c minor and Eb major. This harmonic cycle is treated extremely freely however, particularly in the third movement. As a matter of fact, what strikes me most about these movements is that they are generally the freest in structure of any I have ever written. The second, slow movement, is a canon in Eb minor involving, near the end of the movement, seven separate voices.

Cello Counterpoint is one of the most difficult pieces I have ever written, calling for extremely tight, fast-moving rhythmic relationships.

The piece is a little more than 11 minutes in duration, and was co-commissioned by the Koussevitzky Foundation in the Library of Congress, the Royal Conservatory in The Hague and Leiden University, for cellist Maya Beiser.

– Steve Reich

Anmerkungen des Komponisten

Cello Counterpoint (2003) ist für acht Celli geschrieben und kann von einem Solisten gespielt werden. Aufnahmen der anderen Instrumente sind als Leihgabe von der Boosey & Hawkes Verleihbibiliothek zu erstehen. Alternativ kann das Stück auch von einem Cello Oktett gespielt werden. Bitte beachten Sie, dass es Unterschiede in der Verteilung der Teile zwischen der Version für Solo Cello mit Aufnahmeband und der Version für Cello Oktett einschließlich des 1. Cellos gibt. Es werden unterschiedliche Materialien verwendet werden, wenn das Solo-Cello zum Aufnahmeband gespielt wird. Es beinhaltet ebenso Teile um Ihr eigenes Playback zu erstellen, falls Sie es wünschen.

Cello Counterpoint ist in drei Sätzen geschrieben (schnell, langsam, schnell). Der erste und letzte Satz basieren beide auf ähnlichem Akkordzyklus, der sich mehrdeutig zwischen c-Moll und Es-Dur hin und her bewegt. Dieser harmonische Zyklus wird extrem frei behandelt, ganz besonders jedoch im dritten Satz. In der Tat, was mich an diesen Bewegungen am meisten bewegt ist, dass sie wohl die freieste Struktur besitzt von all denen, die ich bisher geschrieben habe. Der zweite Satz ist von langsamer Natur. Es ist ein in Es-Moll geschriebener Kanon, der gegen Ende des Satzes sieben Stimmen beinhaltet.

Cello Counterpoint ist eines der schwierigsten Stücke, die ich je geschrieben habe. Es beinhaltet sehr schnell bewegende rhythmische Beziehungen.

Das Stück dauert ein bisschen länger als 11 Minuten und wurde von der Koussevitzky–Stiftung der Bibiliothek des Kongresses, dem königliche Konservatorium in Den Haag und der Leiden University für Cellistin Maya Beiser in Auftrag gegeben.

– Steve Reich

Note du compositeur

Cello Counterpoint (2003), pour huit violoncelles, peut être exécuté par un soliste accompagné des autres parties préenregistrées. Cet enregistrement est disponible en matériel de location auprès des éditions Boosey & Hawkes. Cette pièce peut également être jouée par un octuor de violoncelles. On notera qu'il existe quelques divergences dans la distribution des parties entre la version pour violoncelle et enregistrement et la version pour octuor de violoncelles incluant une partie de Violoncelle I. On utilisera un matériel différent (comportant des parties permettant de réaliser un enregistrement en propre si on le souhaite) pour l'exécution de la version pour violoncelle solo et enregistrement.

Cello Counterpoint suit un schéma en trois mouvements : vif – lent – vif. Le premier et le dernier mouvements sont tous deux construits sur le même cycle de quatre accords qui se meut de façon ambiguë en allers et retours entre *do* mineur et *mib* majeur. Ce cycle harmonique est, toutefois, traité de manière extrêmement libre, surtout dans le troisième mouvement. De fait, ce qui me frappe le plus dans ces mouvements est qu'ils représentent les structures les plus libres que j'ai jamais écrites. Le deuxième mouvement lent est un canon en *mib* mineur comportant, vers la fin du mouvement, sept voix séparées.

Cello Counterpoint est l'une de mes pièces les plus difficiles et exige des rapports rythmiques extrêmement serrés et rapides.

D'une durée d'un peu plus de 11 minutes, cette pièce répondit à une commande conjointe de la Fondation Koussevitzky de la Bibliothèque du Congrès, du Conservatoire Royal de La Haye et de l'Université de Leiden pour la violoncelliste Maya Beiser.

– Steve Reich

First performed October 18, 2003 at the
Krannert Center, University of Illinois,
Champaign-Urbana, IL, Maya Beiser, cello

Recorded by Maya Beiser
on Nonesuch 79891-2

Duration: ca. 11½ minutes

*Performance materials are available from
the Boosey & Hawkes Rental Library*

CELLO COUNTERPOINT

Solo Cello

STEVE REICH

I.

979-0-051-09827-9

Printed in USA
Printed 2020

V.S.

II.

V.S.